DISCOVER our AMAZING WORLD

7 ENGINEERING WONDERS OF THE MODERN WORLD

Virginia Evans
Jenny Dooley

Express Publishing

Contents

Introduction

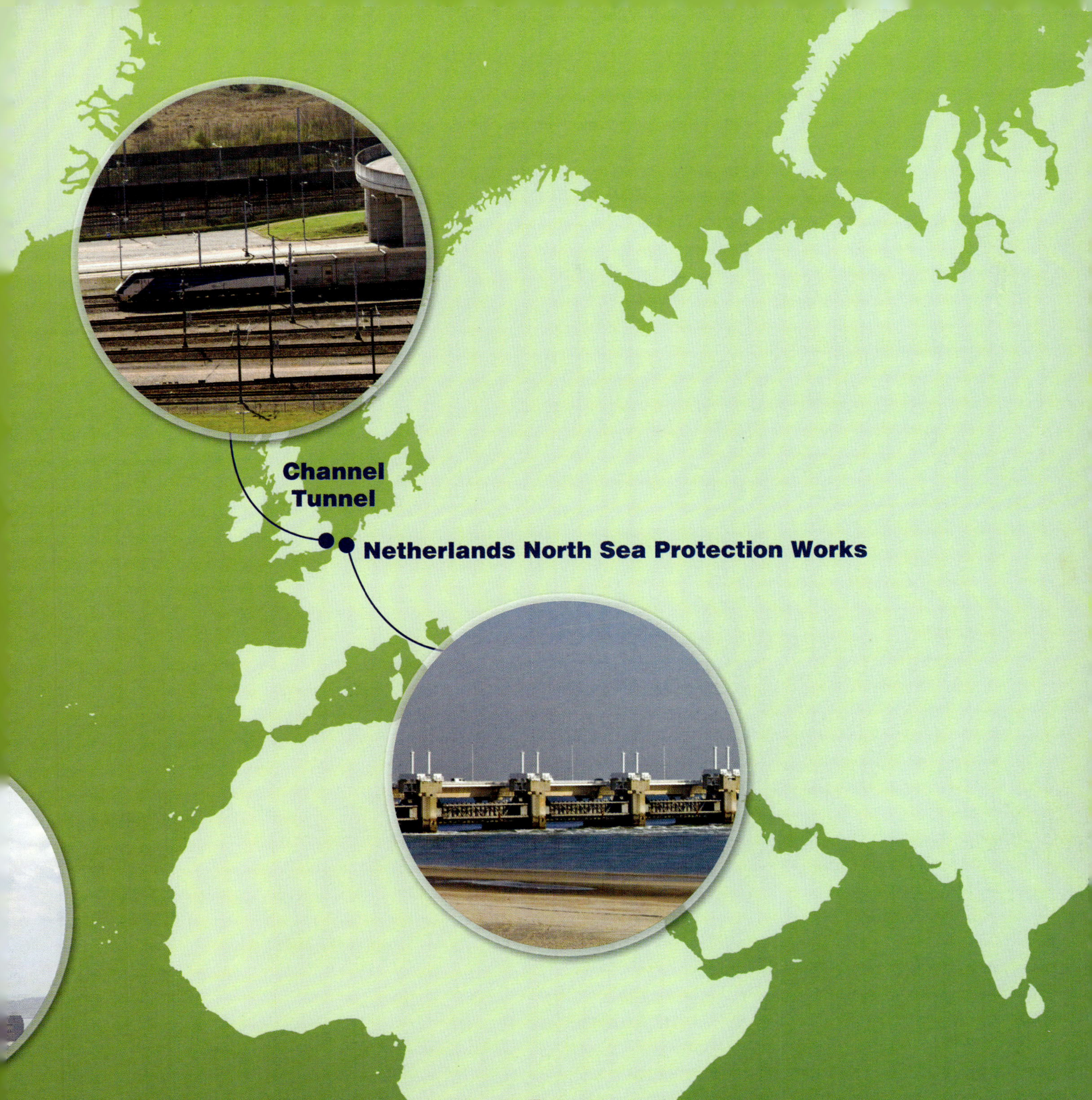

The seven modern wonders of the world, recognized by the American Society of Civil Engineers, are the seven greatest civil engineering achievements of the 20th century. They are wonderful because of their architectural greatness. They are special because they showcase modern man's ability to do the impossible. Each one has a positive impact on the world and is both a monument and an incredible feat of construction.

The CN Tower

The CN Tower in Toronto, Canada, is a telecommunications tower which broadcasts over 20 television, radio, and wireless signals across the city and even further into the province of Ontario.

The city of Toronto was in a building boom in the 1960s. All of a sudden, new skyscrapers were being erected towards the heavens. However, these impressive tall buildings blocked radio and TV signals in the city and made it difficult to move data between businesses. The Canadian National Railway (CN) decided to build a tall communications tower to tackle this problem. The tower had to be tall enough so that radio or TV signals would not be obstructed by other high-rise buildings.

Construction of the CN Tower got under way on February 6, 1973. A huge hole was dug in the ground to make the tower's foundation. Then, a 22-foot (6.7 meter) thick base made from concrete and reinforced with steel bars was put inside the hole. The tower built from these foundations was also made of concrete, which was mixed on site and pumped into the form. A massive total of 53,000 cubic yards (40,500 cubic meters) of concrete was poured into the form during the tower's construction. The CN Tower was constructed at an amazing rate of 18 feet per day. It was finished at a cost of $63 million and opened to the public on June 26, 1976.

The CN Tower became the world's tallest free-standing structure in 1976 breaking the record held by the Ostankino Tower in Moscow (1,772 feet - 540 meters).

It remained the world's tallest free-standing structure until 2007, when the world's current tallest building was built - Burj Khalifa (2,716 feet - 828 meters) in Dubai, United Arab Emirates.

A major feat of engineering

The construction of the tower was a major feat of engineering in its own right. Construction began in 1973. Workers dug down 49 feet (15 meters) deep at the site of the CN Tower in order to lay the building's foundations.

It went up at a rate of 18 feet (6 meters) per day and the engineers used an aircraft-type bombsight to make sure the tower stayed perfectly straight as it was being built. The designers also used a wind tunnel to help them in the design of the tower to ensure that the strong winds at the top would not be a problem. Engineers also attached two 10-ton counterweights to the mast so that the tower wouldn't sway too much.

The construction company bought an old US military helicopter which was used to hoist the antenna to the top of the tower.

The tower has a wide base and gradually becomes thinner the higher it gets. More than halfway up the tower at 1,122 feet (342 meters) is a large, round pod. This is the main part of the tower and has seven stories. It was built around the base of the tower and lifted up into place as one piece. Inside are restaurants, shops, observation decks, and technical equipment. The rest of the tower is empty except for the elevators and stairwells. There is also a smaller observation deck higher than the main one, at 1,465 feet (446.5 meters). This is called the SkyPod and is located just below the tower's metal antenna.

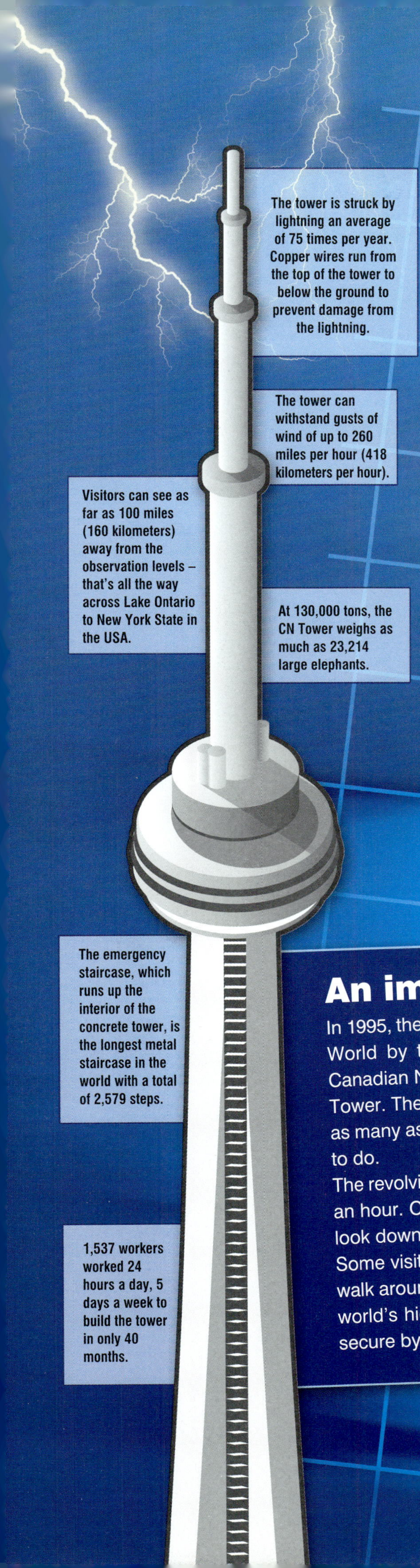

An important symbol

In 1995, the CN Tower was declared one of the Seven Wonders of the Modern World by the American Society of Civil Engineers. Despite the fact the Canadian National Railway sold the tower in 1995, it is still known as the CN Tower. The tower is one of Canada's most important symbols and it attracts as many as 1.5 million visitors every year. It offers plenty of things for visitors to do.

The revolving restaurant on the main deck completes a full circle in little over an hour. One of the observation levels has a glass floor to allow visitors to look down on the city far below.

Some visitors take advantage of the thrilling EdgeWalk where people can walk around the 5-foot (1.5-meter) wide metal roof of the main pod. It's the world's highest outdoor, full-circle, hands-free walk, but visitors are kept secure by a safety rope which is tied to an overhead rail system.

Word Bank & Activities pp. 34-35

The Channel **Tunnel**

One hundred years ago, to get from England to France, someone had to take a boat or a plane. There was no other way to do it. As recently as the 1980s, ferries were still the easiest way to make this trip. Since 1994, however, there has been another way. The Channel Tunnel is actually composed of three underground passages – a service tunnel and two railway tunnels that take people and their vehicles under the English Channel. The trip is faster than a ferry, only taking about thirty-five minutes to get from Folkestone, Kent, in England, to Coquelles, Pas-de-Calais, in France. The Channel Tunnel is the longest undersea tunnel in the entire world. It is 31 miles (50.5 kilometers) long, and 24 miles (37.9 kilometers) of it are under the sea at an average depth of 147 feet (45 meters). The tunnels are 25 feet (7.6 meters) in diameter and made of concrete.

Old Channel crossing ideas

The idea of a tunnel across the English Channel was not new. The first person to propose this idea was a French engineer called Albert Mathieu. In 1802, Mathieu showed his plan to Napoleon Bonaparte, the emperor of France. Mathieu's plans consisted of two underwater tunnels with an artificial island halfway between the two countries. Mathieu also included ventilation shafts throughout the tunnel. He planned to have horse-drawn carriages take people and cargo through his tunnel. Napoleon liked the plans for the tunnel a lot, but nothing ever came of it.

In 1834 another Frenchman, Aimé Thomé de Gamond, revived Mathieu's idea of connecting England and France. He spent lots of time studying the land and geographical features around the two shores and even dived underwater to examine the sea floor. His plan was to create a mined railway tunnel with a station in the middle of the Channel. His proposal interested both countries' rulers, but political differences meant that the plans were abandoned.

In the 20th century, talk of a tunnel beneath the Channel once again rose to the surface. In 1985, four groups submitted proposals to French and English leaders. Three never saw the light of day. One of the proposals was to build a 13-mile (21 kilometer) tunnel connected with artificial islands and bridges. Another plan involved large road tunnels with ventilation towers which would rise high above the surface of the sea. The third was for a 2.8-mile (4.5 kilometer) wide suspension bridge for road transport. Despite public opinion favoring a tunnel through which people could drive their vehicles, officials decided to accept the fourth plan, which was to become the Channel Tunnel. It was decided that a railway tunnel would be safer and easier to maintain.

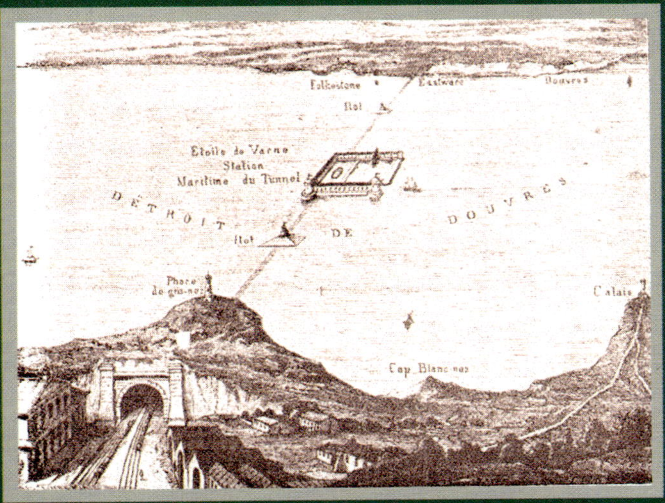

Ten workers were killed during the construction of the tunnel between 1987 and 1993.

Constructing the tunnel

Over 13,000 skilled and unskilled workers were hired for the construction of the tunnels, which began in 1987. With a team starting on either side, the plan was to meet below the seabed in the middle of the channel. First, giant drills were used to make holes through the hard rock underground. Then, 11 different tunnel boring machines were used to create three tunnels, one for train travel in each direction, and a service tunnel in the middle, which was completed before the other two. Digging the tunnel was a little more difficult on the French side, because the rock below the seabed was weaker and more permeable than the rock on the English side. This meant that water was able to leak through the rock more easily, and danger of the tunnel caving in was higher. For these reasons, construction on the French side had to be carried out more slowly than on the English side. All the rock that was dug up was carried out of the tunnels. On the English side this debris was used to construct the train station and a park. On the French side, the rock was used to extend the French coastline ever so slightly. When it finally opened in 1994, the Channel Tunnel project was 80% over budget.

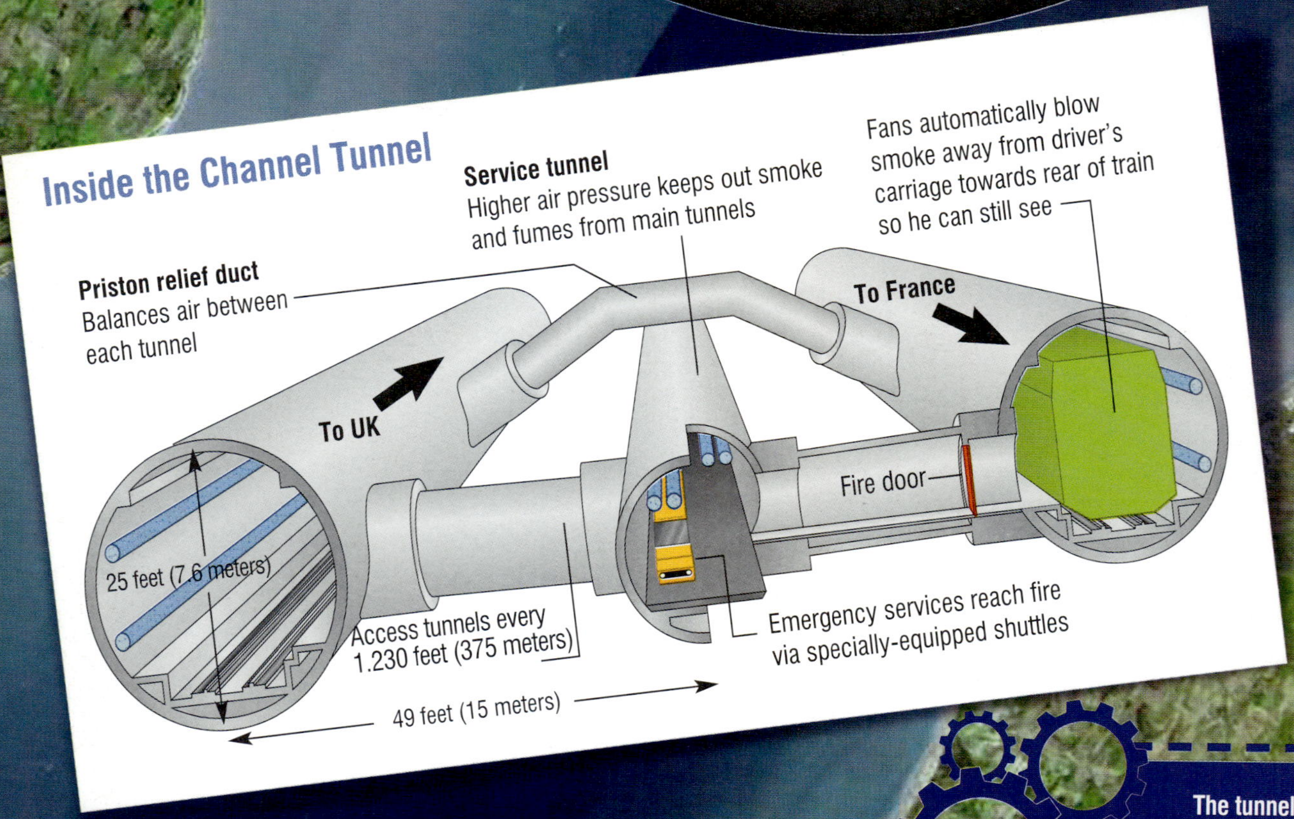

The tunnel was 80% over budget.

Open for business

After almost 150 years of plans and dreams, the Channel Tunnel opened. Today, people are able to travel from London to Paris in about two hours without switching trains. In addition, people are able to drive their cars onto the train and take their vehicles with them to France or England. Freight trains use the tracks, too. The Channel Tunnel continues to become more popular, proving that men like Mathieu and de Gamond were simply ahead of their time.

Word Bank & Activities pp. 36-37

The Empire **State Building**

At 1,454 feet (443 meters) high, the Empire State Building is the most famous and recognizable skyscraper in the world. This iconic building was also the tallest in the world for more than 40 years. With 103 stories, it is one of New York City's landmarks and has been a symbol of the city's skyline for over 80 years. Over 3 million visitors come to the Empire State Building every year.

The most impressive feature of the Empire State Building, however, is the fact it took only one year and 45 days to complete, and that was without any overtime. Not only that, but the building was so well-constructed that in 1945, it was easily repaired after a large B-25 bomber plane crashed into it under thick fog. The quick and efficient construction of the Empire State Building was set to revolutionize the construction of high-rise buildings for years to come. Despite no longer being the world's tallest building, the Empire State building remains the standard against which all modern skyscrapers are judged.

A race to the top

In the 1920s and 1930s, there was an informal competition to build the tallest building in the world. New technological advances made it possible to build taller and taller structures. One of the most important of these was the elevator. Another important innovation was a new building technique called steel frame construction which allowed buildings to support more weight.

The views from the observatory, which is 1,224 feet (373 meters) from the ground, are the most popular with visitors to the city.

The Empire State Building was the first building to have more than 100 floors.

Two other Manhattan construction projects, 40 Wall Street and the Chrysler Building, were being built in attempts to become the world's tallest building when construction work began on the Empire State Building. Each building held the title for less than one year until the Empire State Building was completed.

In 1930, the Chrysler Building became the tallest building in the world, a record that would last for less than a year. A businessman by the name of John Jacob Raskob and the former governor of New York, Al Smith, decided to go into business together, determined to make an even taller building. Architect William F. Lamb created a design in just two weeks based on existing buildings in North Carolina and Ohio – only much taller. Raskob and Smith liked the Art Deco design, and work soon began on what would become the Empire State Building. Construction went remarkably well, with 3,400 men perched high above the city, riveting steel beams into place. The majority of workers were European immigrants, but hundreds of Native Americans were hired as well. All the building materials came from other parts of the country, and were sent to the construction site ready to be put in place.

The building took a little over 410 days to complete, and cost barely over half of what was estimated at just less than $25 million. The official opening was on May 1, 1931, when President Herbert Hoover turned on the building's lights by pushing a button in Washington D.C.

This famous photograph by Lewis Hine shows a construction worker on the steel frame of the Empire State Building with the Chrysler Building in the background.

A famous landmark

When it first opened, the Empire State Building did not make a lot of money. For a while, people called it the "Empty State Building." This was due to the fact that few businesses rented office space in it because the building was far from subway stations and bus lines. In its first years of operation, the building made as much money from visitors as it did from business. Despite being the tallest building in the world from 1931 until 1972, being tall did not pay the bills. Today, offices on all 85 floors are filled, but the building still relies primarily on its popularity with tourists, who buy tickets to the observation deck on the 86th floor. The remaining 16 floors make up the Art Deco tower, which is topped by the observatory on the 102nd floor. The Empire State Building is one of the United States' most popular buildings.

Word Bank & Activities pp. 38-39

The Golden **Gate Bridge**

Open since May, 1937, the 8,981-foot (2,737 meter) long Golden Gate Bridge, once the world's longest and tallest suspension bridge, is one of the world's most photographed icons. This orange-vermilion suspension bridge spans the strait that connects the bay to the Pacific Ocean. The bridge connects the city of San Francisco, California to Marin County to the north. It provides a way for people to get between these places quickly by car, but it also allows for travel on foot and by bicycle.

The bridge combines engineering strength and beauty. It hangs from two 746-foot (227 meter) high steel towers, and is suspended by two massive main cables that contain 80,000 miles (128,748 kilometers) of wire and measure over 3 feet (1 meter) in diameter. In fact, the Golden Gate Bridge cables contain enough wire to go around the planet three times. The bridge survived the 1989 Loma Prieta earthquake without damage and it has only been shut briefly to traffic three times due to periods of high sustaining winds since it opened - the longest closure being 3 hours and 27 minutes long.

A difficult task

Before the bridge was built, the only way to get across the Golden Gate Strait was by boat. Although people had wanted to build a bridge across this body of water, the area was not ideal for a bridge. The strait itself is over 370 feet (113 meters) deep, and area around the strait is windy and foggy. For this reason, it was a long time before the Golden Gate Bridge could be built.

A large team of people worked together to design and build the bridge. One of these people, Leon Moisseiff, also designed the Manhattan Bridge in New York City. Construction workers braved the high winds, thick fog, and dizzying heights, and completed the bridge in four years. During that time, only eleven men died – a great accomplishment at the time. This was thanks to a vast safety net that chief engineer Joseph Strauss suspended under the bridge.

Charles Ellis was a structural engineer who worked very closely with Leon Moesseiff on the bridge design. But before construction even began, Ellis was fired because of an argument with Joseph Strauss. By this point, Ellis was so interested in the bridge's success that he kept working on the bridge for free. He played a large role in the bridge's design, even though he was not on the payroll. The engineering drawings in the Library of Congress have his signature on them, but Strauss took the credit. Finally, in 2007, officials gave Ellis formal credit for his technical and theoretical work on the design of the bridge.

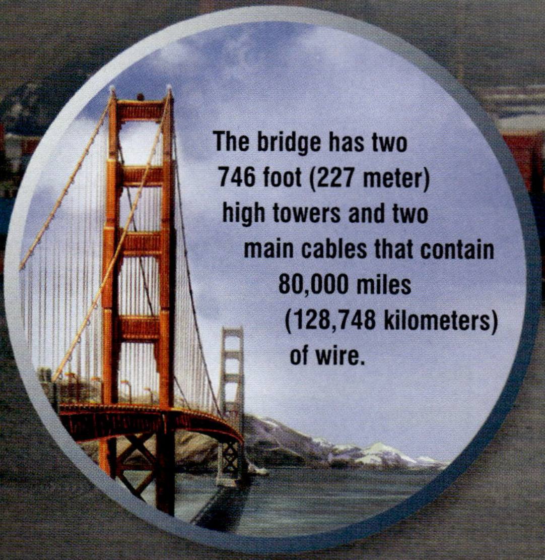

The bridge has two 746 foot (227 meter) high towers and two main cables that contain 80,000 miles (128,748 kilometers) of wire.

Why is the bridge not golden?

The Bridge has never been painted gold despite its name. It is orange-vermilion, also known as 'International Orange' because the bright color provides better visibility for passing ships, particularly as this part of the bay is prone to low clouds and thick fog.

A busy route

Today, over 100,000 cars cross the steel bridge each day. This does not count the people who cross on bicycles or on foot. A $6 toll helps pay for the maintenance of the bridge, including painting touch-ups. A dedicated team of 200 iron workers and painters are responsible for working on the bridge. They help keep this landmark safe and looking nice for the many people who use it each day.

- The lanes of traffic on the Golden Gate Bridge change depending on traffic patterns.

Word Bank & Activities pp. 40-41

The Itaipu Dam

The Itaipu Dam is 5 miles (8 kilometres) wide. It spans the Paraná River at the border between Brazil and Paraguay in South America, and is the largest hydroelectric dam and power facility in the entire world. The reservoir behind the dam covers an area of 521 square miles (1,350 square kilometers).

The dam is actually made of four different dams joined together. There is an earth fill dam, a rock fill dam, and both the main and wing dams are constructed from concrete. The main dam is 643 feet (196 meters) high and is composed of hollow concrete segments which are reinforced with iron and steel.

The main purpose of the Itaipu Dam is to generate electricity. The powerhouse contains 20 53-foot (16 meter) wide hydroelectric generators which are partly submerged underwater. As much as 160 tons of water can pour into each turbine every second, which can generate an amazing 14,000 megawatts of energy – enough to power New York City. Itaipu supplies 17% of all electrical energy in Brazil and 73% of Paraguay's total energy consumption.

Itaipu means "the singing stone" in the Guarani language.

A huge project

After several years of planning, work on the project began in 1975. First, workers redirected the course of the 8th longest river in the world. They dug a 1.3-mile (2 kilometer) bypass around the construction site, which removed 50 million tons of earth and rock. When it was ready, the workers let the river change its path, and construction of the dam began. Workers poured concrete at an amazing pace. Each day, they used enough concrete to build 24 ten-story buildings. Once the concrete work was done, electrical equipment was transported and installed.

In 1982, workers allowed the river to flow back on its original course. This time, however, a huge wall of concrete was blocking the flow of the water. It took fourteen days to fill up the reservoir. At an official opening ceremony on November 5, 1982, the presidents of Brazil and Paraguay inaugurated the dam together.

The dam is as high as a 65-story building.

The blackout

On November 10, 2009, after 10 pm, a power outage occurred throughout a large part of Brazil and, for a short time, the whole of Paraguay. Between 60 and 80 million people were affected by the blackout, which happened when transmission from the power plant at Itaipu was disrupted. This blacked out the whole country of Paraguay for 15 minutes, and plunged large Brazilian cities such as Rio de Janeiro and São Paulo into darkness.

The worst affected areas were Brazil's southeast regions, but most areas were affected in some way. Just over two hours later, power was restored to most areas, but some residents of Sao Paulo had to wait six hours before they had their power back.

The power outage in 2009 was the first and only failure in the Itaipu Dam's history. Experts believe that heavy rains and strong winds caused a short circuit in one of the dam's transmission lines and resulted in the instant loss of 14 gigawatts of power. Other than this one power failure, the dam is incredibly successful. Not only does it provide power to Brazil and Paraguay, it is also a popular tourist attraction in the area.

The amount of steel used in the Itaipu Dam is enough to construct 300 Eiffel Towers.

Word Bank & Activities pp. 42-43

The North Sea **Protection Works**

The Netherlands North Sea Protection Works is not one structure, but rather it is a vast and complex series of dams, dikes, storm barriers and floodgates which protect the Netherlands from the force of the North Sea.

Nearly a third of the land in the Netherlands is below sea level, but as this small, northern European country is located on the southern part of the North Sea, the Dutch have always been concerned about the hazards of major flooding in their country. For as long as the area has been settled, people have worked to overcome the threatening sea.

In earlier times, people built their homes on higher land and later built dams out of earth. It was not until the 20th century, however, that people possessed technology advanced enough to build the defenses against flooding the Netherlands has today. The North Sea Protection Works consists of two important phases which have been vital in holding back the sea: the Zuiderzee Works and the Delta Works.

The Zuiderzee Works

The Zuiderzee, which literally means "Southern Sea" in Dutch, was a shallow bay of the North Sea. It was 20 miles (32 kilometers) long and 30 miles (48 kilometers) wide. It covered an area of 2,000 square miles (5,180 square kilometers), but it was only about 15 feet (4.6 meters) deep. This bay often flooded the surrounding land. In 1421, it flooded 72 villages, killing about 10,000 people. In the 17th century, the first plans to address the Zuiderzee problem were drawn up. In 1927, work began on a 19-mile (30-kilometer) long dam. Ships were used to dump large quantities of dirt in two parallel lines in the bay. In between the two mounds of dirt, the ships dumped sand, and then more dirt, stones and branches were put on top of everything. When the dam was finished, it separated the North Sea from the Zuiderzee.

The Delta Works

The aim of the Delta Works was to control the flow of water where the mouths of the Meuse and Rhine Rivers form a delta. The fishermen living in the affected areas were very upset, since they worried about losing access to the sea. Engineers came up with a solution that would be able to safeguard the area from flooding and still allow access to the sea. They designed a 2-mile (3.2 kilometer) long moving gate system that allows fishing boats to pass, and only closes when storm surges threaten the coast. It is called the Maeslant Barrier.

Today, there is still a body of water where the Zuiderzee used to be. It is not saltwater, though. Instead, it is a freshwater lake, called IJsselmeer.

Not over yet

To this day, the Netherlands North Sea Protection Works are in place. These projects are some of the most amazing engineering achievements in the entire world. The men and women who worked on them have conquered one of nature's greatest forces – the sea. The work isn't over yet. The Delta Commission recommends huge improvements to the North Sea Protection Works because of global warming. If the estimates of rising sea levels are correct, the existing works will not be effective in the future. To this end, the Dutch government plans to spend a lot of time and money improving the system.

The Delta Works took over 40 years to complete.

Word Bank & Activities pp. 44-45

The Panama Canal

To get from the Atlantic to the Pacific Ocean before 1914, ships either had to travel 8,000 miles (12,875 kilometers) around the coast of South America, or through the dangerous Straits of Magellan. In 1914, however, everything changed when the Panama Canal opened and allowed ships to pass from the Atlantic Ocean to the Pacific Ocean. The French attempted to construct a canal in 1881. The same man who created the Suez Canal, Ferdinand de Lesseps, was in charge of the project, but the attempt failed. The cost and difficulty of the project proved too high.

In 1904, US President Theodore Roosevelt bought the French equipment and the rights to build the canal.

The Americans employed over 56,000 people during the construction and almost 6,000 died as a result of accidents and disease.

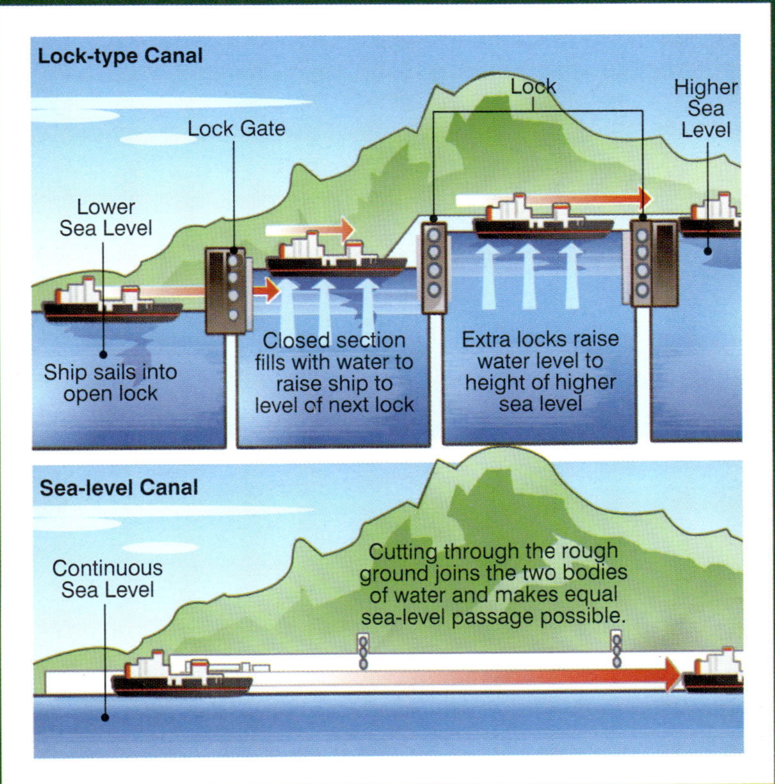

The French engineers had attempted to build a canal that stayed at sea level for the entire width of the Isthmus of Panama. Though the distance across was less than 50 miles, the difficult landscape included dense jungles and rocky mountains. To keep the canal at sea level required extensive excavation of this rugged terrain.

When the American engineers took over, they proposed a different solution. They designed a canal with a series of structures called locks, which work like a staircase. The ship sails into the first lock. When the lock doors close, water is allowed into the lock until the ship rises to the water level in the next lock. The ship can then pass to the next lock, and repeat the process.

Construction

Construction began in 1904. The French attempt had suffered from workers dying from diseases such as yellow fever and malaria, both caused by mosquito bites. So, when the Americans started the project, they invested a lot of money in sanitation and reducing the threat of mosquitos. They built new houses for the workers which had screens to keep insects out.

The American plan included damming the Chagres River to create an artificial lake called Lake Gatun. Ships entering from the Atlantic Ocean would go through s series of three locks to raise them to the 85-foot level of the lake. They would then sail across the 85 mile lake, up a section of the Chagres River, and through a man-made section of the canal called the Gaillard Cut. The Gaillard Cut is considered an engineering masterpiece because a valley had to be cut out of a mountain to create the passageway. At that point, another set of locks lowered the ship down to the level of Miraflores Lake, another artificial lake 54 feet above sea level. A short mile-long sail across the lake brought ships to the final set of locks where they

would be at the level of the Pacific Ocean and could sail out into the open sea.

The Americans used the Panama Railway to move all the dirt from the excavation process. A total of 115 train engines and 2,300 train carriages were used to carry the dirt. 102 rail-mounted steam shovels were used to carry out the digging. The canal cost $375 million which was $23 million less than the government had predicted in 1907. The project was completed two years ahead of schedule and officially opened on August 15, 1914.

A great passageway

In 1999, Panama got control of the canal for the first time. Today, more ships than ever pass through the canal, about 13,000 per year. A plan to add another set of locks on the Pacific Ocean side of the canal is currently in place. It is certain that this engineering feat will be useful for years to come.

The first ship to transit Panama Canal was the S.S. Ancon on August 15, 1914, shortly after (World War I) had broken out in Europe.

At this time, the largest size of ship that is allowed through the Panama Canal is called Panamax. It can be no more than 365 feet (289 meters) long and 107 feet (32 meters) wide.

Word Bank & Activities pp. 46-47

Introduction/The CN Tower

Word Bank

(pp. 4-7)

wonder (n) = a phenomenon

recognize (v) = to accept

engineer (n) = a professional who designs large structures such as roads and bridges

civil engineering (n) = the planning, design and construction of public buildings, bridges, roads, etc.

architectural (adj) = related to architecture, including buildings or other man-made constructions

greatness (n) = importance

positive (adj) = beneficial

impact (n) = an effect

monument (n) = a memorial

incredible (adj) = amazing

feat (n) = an achievement

construction (n) = creation, building

telecommunications tower (phr) = a tall structure which houses electrical equipment used to send and receive signals and messages

broadcast (v) = to transmit

wireless signals (phr) = radio waves that are sent through the air, without requiring the use of cables

province (n) = a region

building boom (phr) = a sharp increase in construction activity

erect (v) = to raise

the heavens (n) = the sky

impressive (adj) = striking

block (v) = to hinder

radio signals (phr) = electromagnetic waves used to send and receive messages

data (n) = information

tackle (v) = to handle

obstruct (v) = to stop, to block

high-rise building (phr) = a tall building with many floors

get under way (phr) = to start happening

dig (v) = to make a hole in the ground

foundation (n) = an underground structure supporting a building

base (n) = bottom

concrete (n) = a type of very strong building material

reinforce (v) = to provide extra strength and support

steel bar (phr) = a rod of very strong metal consisting of iron

on site (phr) = at the place where works are held

pump (v) = to inject

form (n) = a structure

massive (adj) = huge

total (n) = a whole

cubic meter (phr) = a unit of measuring volume that is equal to 1000 liters

pour (v) = to make a liquid flow

rate (n) = pace

remain (v) = to continue being

free-standing (adj) = standing on its own, not supported by walls, etc.

current (adj) = present

break the record (phr) = to beat a previously considered high achievement by doing even better

(pp. 8-9)

in its own right (phr) = having obtained or achieved sth because of its own merits, without depending on sth else

lay (v) = to put down

bombsight (n) = a mechanism used by aircraft in order to drop bombs accurately

wind tunnel (phr) = a tool used to examine the impact of air moving past solid structures

ensure (v) = to make sure

attach (v) = to connect

counterweight (n) = a heavy mass that provides balance against something that is equally heavy

mast (n) = a long pole that supports radio or television aerials

sway (v) = to move from side to side

military (adj) = related to the armed forces

hoist (v) = to lift

antenna (n) = an aerial

gradually (adv) = little by little

pod (n) = a long narrow area

story (n) = level, floor

observation deck (phr) = a platform usually constructed on a tall building from where people can admire views from high up

elevator (n) = a lift

stairwell (n) = the part of a building where the stairs are

strike (v) = to hit

lightning (n) = flashes of light seen in the sky during a storm

copper wire (phr) = thin thread made out of a reddish brown metal

prevent (v) = to stop from happening

withstand (v) = to resist

gust of wind (phr) = a sudden, strong burst of wind

emergency staircase (phr) = stairs people use to exit a building in the event of danger

interior (n) = the inside of a structure

symbol (n) = a representation of sth

declare (v) = to announce officially

attract (v) = to draw towards an area or activity

revolving (adj) = rotating

thrilling (adj) = exciting

secure (adj) = safe

safety rope (phr) = a thick cord used to protect sb from injury

overhead (adj) = above one's head

rail system (phr) = a set of train tracks

Pre-Reading activities

1 **a) How much do you know about the CN Tower? Decide which of the following statements are *T* (true) or *F* (false).**

1 The CN Tower was built in the 1970s. ....
2 The CN Tower is today the tallest building in the world. ....
3 There are offices in the CN Tower. ....
4 The design of the CN Tower makes it resistant to very strong winds. ....
5 Visitors can do some shopping and have dinner in the CN Tower. ....
6 Visitors must stay inside the CN Tower at all times. ....

b) Listen, read, and check.

While-Reading activities

2 **Match the beginnings of the sentences to their endings.**

1 ☐ The CN Tower was built in order to
2 ☐ A military tool was used so as to
3 ☐ A helicopter was required to
4 ☐ The higher up the tower gets,
5 ☐ The tower's emergency metal staircase
6 ☐ During the EdgeWalk, people can

A ensure the tower remained straight during its construction.
B make a full circle around the tower's main pod.
C is the longest of its kind in the world.
D allow the unobstructed broadcast of TV and radio signals.
E the thinner it becomes.
F lift the aerial to the top of the tower.

3 **SUBJECT-SPECIFIC VOCABULARY: Choose the correct item.**

1 **Copper wires/Steel bars** were used to reinforce the base of the tower.
2 **Counterweights/Wind tunnels** ensure that the tower doesn't sway too much.
3 The tower sends out wireless **signals/data** across a wide area.
4 A helicopter was used to place the 335-foot long communications **pod/antenna** on top of the tower.
5 In order to lay the **foundations/masts** of the tower, workers dug 49 feet into the ground.

After-Reading activities

4 **Answer the following questions.**

1 What materials were used in the construction of the base of the CN Tower?

....

2 When was the Tower's record as the world's tallest structure broken?

....

3 What honor was given to the Tower in 1995?

....

4 Why do you think people go on the EdgeWalk?

....

5 **Complete the sentences using information from the text.**

1 The CN Tower was built in order to deal with the problem of tall buildings blocking ....
2 To make the concrete base of the tower stronger, they used ....
3 The main deck of the tower contains ....
4 Copper wires were placed to ensure that .... doesn't damage the tower.
5 It took the huge number of .... workers to complete the tower in just ....
6 Visitors who go on the EdgeWalk are kept safe by being connected to an ....

The Channel Tunnel

Word Bank

(pp. 10-11)

ferry (n) = a boat that carries people and vehicles across an area of water

underground passage (phr) = a path that is below the surface of the Earth

vehicle (n) = a means of transportation

undersea tunnel (phr) = a long, covered passage that is below the surface of the sea

entire (adj) = whole

depth (n) = the distance down from the top to the bottom of sth

diameter (n) = the length of a straight line passing through the center of a circular object

propose (v) = to suggest

emperor (n) = a ruler

consist of (v) = to be made up of

artificial (adj) = man-made

include (v) = to contain

ventilation shaft (phr) = a vertical passage that allows air to go in and out of a place

horse-drawn carriage (phr) = a coach pulled by horses

cargo (n) = goods

revive (v) = to reintroduce

connect (v) = to join

geographical features (phr) = the characteristics of the Earth (e.g. rivers, terrain types, etc.)

shore (n) = coast

dive (v) = to jump into water

sea floor (phr) = the bottom of the sea

mined (adj) = created by digging deep into the ground

station (n) = a place where trains stop to let people on and off

proposal (n) = a suggestion

abandon (v) = to give up

beneath (adv) = below

rise to the surface (phr) = to appear

submit (v) = to present

leader (n) = the head of government

see the light of day (phr) = to appear for the first time

bridge (n) = a structure joining one side of a road, river, etc. to the other

involve (v) = to include

rise (v) = to go up

reject (v) = not to accept

suspension bridge (phr) = a bridge which hangs from strong steel ropes

favor (v) = to prefer

maintain (v) = to keep in good condition

(pp. 12-13)

seabed (phr) = the bottom of the sea

skilled (adj) = able to perform a job well, expert

hire (v) = to employ

drill (n) = a machine used for making holes

boring machine (phr) = a machine used for digging deep holes

service tunnel (phr) = a tunnel from which services such as maintenance, emergency, etc. are run

permeable (adj) = allowing gases or liquid to pass through

leak (v) = to drip or spill through sth

cave in (phr v) = to collapse

construction crew (phr) = a group of workers working on a building site

debris (n) = remains, rubble

extend (v) = to make longer

estimated (adj) = assessed

over budget (phr) = costing more than planned

piston relief duct (phr) = a channel used in keeping the air pressure in two spaces equal

balance (v) = to stabilize

air pressure (phr) = the force applied on a surface or space by the air above

fumes (n) = strong-smelling, unpleasant smoke or gas

fan (n) = a device that has turning blades used to move air

carriage (n) = a section of a train

rear (n) = back

access tunnel (phr) = a passage allowing people in and out of an area

via (prep) = through

shuttle (n) = a vehicle that makes regular trips between two places

equivalent (n) = an equal amount

switch (v) = to swap, to change

freight train (n) = a train that transports goods

be ahead of your time (phr) = to be very advanced

Pre-Reading activities

1 **a) Choose the option that is NOT correct.**

1 The idea of an underwater tunnel across the English Channel was first thought of by
  A the French emperor Napoleon Bonaparte.
  B Albert Mathieu, a French engineer.

2 The plans for an underwater water connection between France and England were originally put aside because
  A the two governments were in disagreement.
  B the estimated cost seemed too high at the time.

3 During the construction of the Channel Tunnel,
  A the English did not know how to make use of the debris.
  B the French faced more difficulties than the English.

4 The total cost of the Channel Tunnel was
  A higher than expected. **B** lower than expected.

b) **Listen, read, and check.**

While-Reading activities

2 **Read the text and choose the correct answer A, B, C or D.**

1 The feature of the Channel Tunnel that makes it unique among other underwater tunnels is
  A its depth. **C** its length.
  B its width. **D** the materials it is made of.

2 The idea of an underwater railway tunnel was first suggested by
  A Napoleon Bonaparte. **C** an English leader.
  B Aimé Thomé de Gamond. **D** Albert Mathieu.

3 Among the proposals presented in the mid 80s, the one that was more popular with the people was that of
  A an underwater tunnel for drivers and their vehicles.
  B a tunnel joined by man-made islands.
  C underwater road tunnels with above-water airing systems.
  D a hanging bridge for vehicles to travel on.

4 The rock on the French side of the constructions was
  A more likely to break and cause a collapse.
  B harder than the rock on the English side.
  C unsuitable to use for any other purposes.
  D used by the French to make parks.

3 **Replace the words/phrases in bold in the sentences below with:** *rubble*, *switch*, *cargo*, *submit*, *maintain*, *rear*.

1 Rail travelers using the Channel Tunnel don't have to **change** trains.

2 A Frenchman was the first to **present** the idea of an underwater link between England and France.

3 Special equipment is used to send smoke towards the **back** of the train.

4 The rocky **debris** that was created during the construction of the Tunnel was put to other uses.

5 Passengers and **goods** are carried through the Tunnel daily.

6 Officials thought that an underwater railway tunnel would be easier to **keep in good condition**.

After-Reading activities

4 **Fill in:** *boring*, *cave in*, *unskilled*, *extended*, *construction*, *budget* **to complete the paragraph summarising the construction of the tunnel.**

A **1)** .... crew of more than 13,000 expert as well as **2)** .... workers started work on the Channel Tunnel in 1987. 11 different **3)** .... machines were required to make the three tunnels. The rock on the French side of the works was not hard enough and engineers feared the ground might **4)** .... With the rock that was left over from the construction, the British built a park and a train station, while the French slightly **5)** .... their coastline. The project came in at 80% over **6)** ....

The Empire State Building

Word Bank

(pp.14-15)

recognizable (adj) = easily identified

iconic (adj) = legendary

landmark (n) = a monument

skyline (n) = the shape created by buildings or mountains against the sky

overtime (n) = extra hours someone puts in at work

bomber plane (phr) = an aircraft which drops bombs

crash (into) (v) = to hit something with extreme force

fog (n) = a very thick cloud close to the ground

efficient (adj) = competent

revolutionize (v) = to transform

high-rise building (phr) = a very tall and modern building

standard (n) = a model, a guideline

skyscraper (n) = a very tall building in the city

judge (v) = to assess

nickname (n) = an informal name

race (n) = a contest

informal (adj) = unofficial

technological advances (phr) = progress in technology

elevator (n) = a lift

innovation (n) = a breakthrough

technique (n) = a method

frame (n) = the basic structure of a building

observatory (n) = an observation deck

attempt (n) = an effort

hold the title (phr) = keep being the best, first, etc.

(pp.16-17)

governor (n) = a political leader in charge of a state or region

determined (adj) = intent, resolute

remarkably (adv) = exceptionally

perched (adj) = sitting in a high position or near the edge of something

rivet (v) = to use short metal pins (rivets) in order to attach pieces of metal together

beam (n) = a long, thick piece of wood, metal, concrete, etc. used in construction

majority (n) = the largest part

immigrant (n) = a person who has moved to a country from a different country

construction site (phr) = an area where a building is being built

opening (n) = a formal event during which something is officially put in operation

button (n) = a small circular object that one presses in order to start something working

background (n) = the scenery behind something

rent (v) = to lease

subway station (phr) = underground railway depot

bus line (phr) = the route followed by a bus

operation (n) = the state of being used, active, open, etc.

bill (n) = money owed for services or goods

rely on (phr v) = to count on

make up (phr v) = to form

Pre-Reading activities

1 **a) Choose the correct option.**

1 The Empire State Building has **eighty floors/one hundred and three floors**.

2 It is visited by over **three million/eighty thousand** people every year.

3 The Empire State Building was built in just **over a year/under two years**.

4 In 1930, the tallest building in the world was **40 Wall Street/The Chrysler Building**.

5 Most of the people employed to work on the construction of the Empire State Building were **European immigrants/Native Americans**.

6 Most of the Empire State Building's income comes from **the rent collected from offices/tickets sold to visitors**.

b) Listen, read, and check.

While-Reading activities

2 **Mark the sentences as *T* (true) or *F* (false).**

1 The Empire State Building was the world's highest building for over four decades. ....

2 A bomb was dropped on the building in 1945. ....

3 It is not clear where the building got ts name from. ....

4 Raskob and Smith really wanted to make a building that looked like the Chrysler Building. ....

5 President Hoover switched on the lights of the Empire State Building from a different location. ....

6 Initially, people did not want to rent office space in the building because it was not close to public transportation services. ....

3 **Fill in:** *observatory*, *frame*, *advances*, *opening*, *beams*, *overtime*.

1 Although the Empire State Building took just over a year to complete, it wasn't required of workers to work .... in order to achieve this.

2 A lot of technological .... in the 1920s and 1930s enabled the construction of taller buildings.

3 The .... of the Empire State Building took place on May 1, 1931.

4 A strong steel .... supports the heavy building.

5 Visitors can enjoy views of the city from the ....

6 The main structure of the building is made up of steel ....

4 **Do the crossword puzzle.**

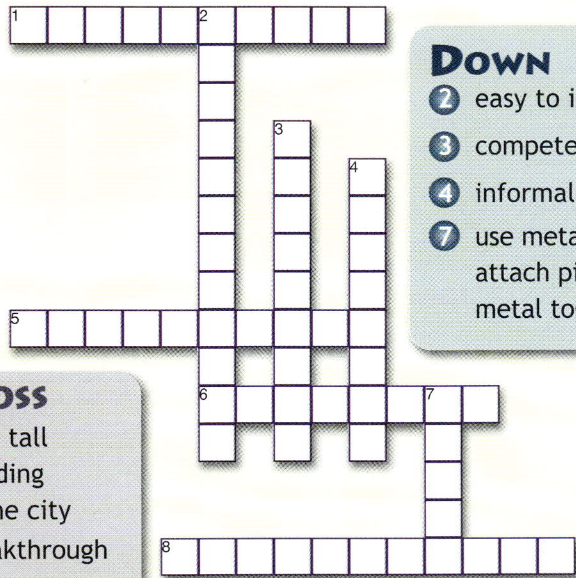

Down

2 easy to identify

3 competent

4 informal name

7 use metal pins to attach pieces of metal together

Across

1 very tall building in the city

5 breakthrough

6 monument

8 observation deck

After-Reading activities

5 ICT **Look up more information on the Empire State Building on the Internet in order to complete the fact sheet below.**

THE EMPIRE STATE BUILDING

General information	
Location:	
Purpose:	
Official website:	
Construction information	
Construction started in:	
Construction completed in:	
Architect:	
Style:	
Technical information	
Total Height (from ground to top of lightning rod):	
Number of floors:	
Number of steps:	
Number of elevators:	
Number of entrances:	

The Golden Gate Bridge

Word Bank

(pp. 18-19)

suspension bridge (phr) = a bridge which hangs from strong steel ropes

icon (n) = a symbol

vermilion (adj) = bright red

span (v) = to extend across an area

strait (n) = a channel

connect (v) = to join

bay (n) = a cove

combine (v) = to mix, to bring together

suspend (v) = to hang

massive (adj) = huge

cable (n) = a strong, thick rope made of wires

contain (v) = to consist of

wire (n) = a thin metal thread

briefly (adv) = for a short time

due to (phr) = because of

sustaining winds (phr) = winds that last for some time

closure (n) = a stop in operation

(pp. 20-21)

task (n) = an assignment

ideal (adj) = perfect

brave (v) = to face

dizzying heights (phr) = very high elevations

accomplishment (n) = an achievement

vast (adj) = huge

safety net (phr) = a large net placed under people working or performing at great height to catch them if they fall

chief (adj) = main

structural engineer (phr) = a professional who examines buildings to detect any problems in the way they are built

fire (v) = to dismiss

payroll (n) = a list of a company's paid employees

take the credit (phr) = to receive praise

official (n) = a person in position of authority

theoretical (adj) = based on ideas relating to a subject

visibility (n) = the distance one can see in particular weather conditions

prone to (adj) = likely to be affected by something

toll (n) = money paid to use a road, bridge, etc.

touch-up (n) = a small addition or repair to something

dedicated (adj) = devoted

lane (n) = a strip of the road in which traffic moves in one direction

traffic pattern (phr) = the characteristic movement and number of vehicles traveling along a road

Pre-Reading activities

1 **a) Choose the appropriate words or phrases from the box below to make true statements about the Golden Gate Bridge.**

• low clouds • by plane • longest and tallest • ten dollars • earthquake • eleven
• six dollars • fire • heavy rain • most photographed • twenty • by boat

1 The Golden Gate Bridge once held the title of being the .... suspension bridge in the world.
2 The bridge did not suffer any damage during the 1989 ....
3 Before the bridge was constructed, people could only travel across the Golden Gate Strait ....
4 .... men died during the four years it took to construct the bridge.
5 The area around the bridge very often gets .... and thick fog.
6 At present, it costs .... to drive your vehicle across the bridge.

b) **Listen, read, and check.**

While-Reading activities

2 **Check the part of the sentence which is true.**

1 The initial objections to building the Golden Gate Bridge had to do with

A ☐ the proposed cost of the project.

B ☐ the unfavorable weather conditions in the area.

2 The number of deaths that occurred during the construction of the bridge was considered

A ☐ surprisingly low.

B ☐ unusually high.

3 Charles Ellis was removed from the project

A ☐ over a disagreement with the chief engineer.

B ☐ because he refused to keep working for free.

4 Eventually, Charles Ellis

A ☐ was put back on the payroll.

B ☐ received the recognition he deserved.

5 The color of the bridge

A ☐ was chosen because it makes the structure easier to see through thick fog.

B ☐ was originally going to be golden, to match the name of the area.

3 **SUBJECT-SPECIFIC VOCABULARY: Label the parts of the suspension bridge with these words:** *anchor point*, *suspender cables*, *deck*, *support towers*, *main cable*, *foundations*.

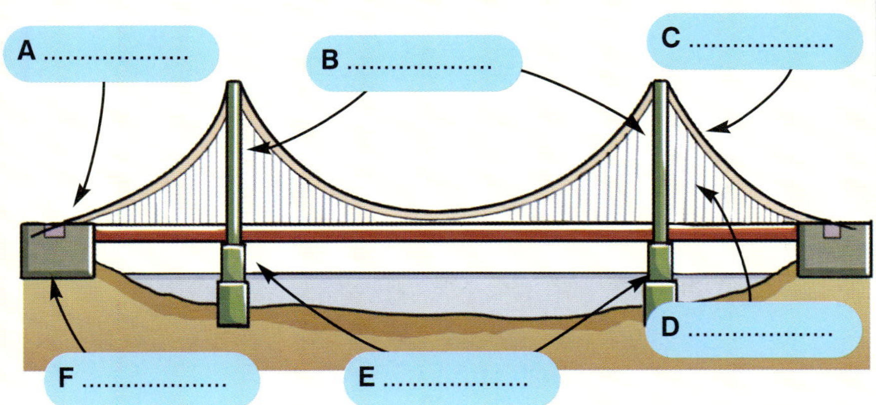

4 **Replace the verbs in bold in the sentences below with:** *suspended*, *combines*, *spans*, *connects*, *fired*.

1 The bridge **joins** the city of San Francisco to Marin County.

2 The bridge **brings together** high standards of construction and design.

3 A huge safety net was **hung** under the bridge for the safety of the workers.

4 Structural engineer Charles Ellis was **dismissed** after arguing with the chief engineer of the project.

5 The Golden Gate Bridge **extends across** the Golden Gate Strait.

After-Reading activities

5 **Use information from the text to complete the fact file on the Golden Gate Bridge.**

THE GOLDEN GATE BRIDGE
Fact File

Location:	
Type:	
Construction began in:	*January, 1933*
Construction ended in:	*April, 1937*
Opened to public in:	
Chief Engineer:	
Total length:	
Width:	*90 ft*
Tower Height:	
Number of lanes:	*6*
Daily traffic:	

6 **ICT** **Look up information on a famous bridge in your country and make a fact file like the one in Ex. 5.**

The Itaipu Dam

Word Bank

(pp. 22-23)

dam (n) = a barrier built across a river in order to stop its flow and collect water

border (n) = a boundary

hydroelectric (adj) = producing electricity using the energy of fast-moving water

power facility (phr) = a factory that produces electricity

reservoir (n) = a man-made lake used for storing water

wing dam (phr) = a barrier that changes the course of a stream

be composed of (phr) = to be formed from

hollow (adj) = empty, unfilled

segment (n) = a section

generate (v) = to produce

powerhouse (n) = a building where electricity is produced

generator (n) = a machine that produces electric power

submerge (v) = to cover with water

turbine (n) = a machine using steam, water, etc. in order to turn a wheel and produce electricity

supply (v) = to provide

energy consumption (phr) = the amount of electricity used by someone

(pp. 24-25)

redirect (v) = to change the direction of something

course (n) = flow

bypass (n) = a channel going around a certain area

pace (n) = speed

install (v) = to put in place

opening ceremony (phr) = a formal celebration to mark the beginning of an event, operation, etc.

activate (v) = to start something working

blackout (n) = a time when an area has no power due to electricity failure

power outage (phr) = an interruption in the supply of electricity

occur (v) = to happen

transmission (n) = transfer

disrupt (v) = to interrupt

plunge (v) = to throw; to sink

strike (v) = to hit

affect (v) = to have an effect on something

restore (v) = to bring back

resident (n) = an inhabitant

failure (n) = when something stops working

short circuit (phr) = a faulty connection in the wiring of electrical equipment

transmission line (phr) = a cable that carries electricity over long distances

result in (phr v) = to cause something to happen

instant (adj) = immediate

loss (n) = the act of losing something

Pre-Reading activities

1 a) Choose the correct option.

1 The Itaipu Dam is **in Brazil/between Paraguay and Brazil**.
2 The name of the dam comes from the **Guarani/Spanish** language.
3 The Paraná River is the eighth **largest/longest** river in the world.
4 Construction work began in **1975/1982**.
5 The dam has the same height as a **56-story/65-story** tall building.
6 During its years of operation, the dam has failed to provide electricity **once/twice**.

b) Listen, read, and check.

While-Reading activities

2 **Match the beginnings of the sentences to their endings.**

1 ☐	The Itaipu Dam provides most of the electricity needed
2 ☐	The dam lies across one of the longest rivers
3 ☐	The generators of the dam
4 ☐	Work on the dam began
5 ☐	The energy generated by the dam is equivalent to the amount used
6 ☐	The 2009 blackout caused total darkness

A by changing the course of the Paraná River.

B by the city of New York.

C in the world.

D in most places in Brazil.

E in Paraguay.

F are partly under water.

3 **SUBJECT-SPECIFIC VOCABULARY: Label the parts of the hydroelectric power station with these words:** *transmission lines*, *control gate*, *reservoir*, *turbine*, *powerhouse*, *dam*.

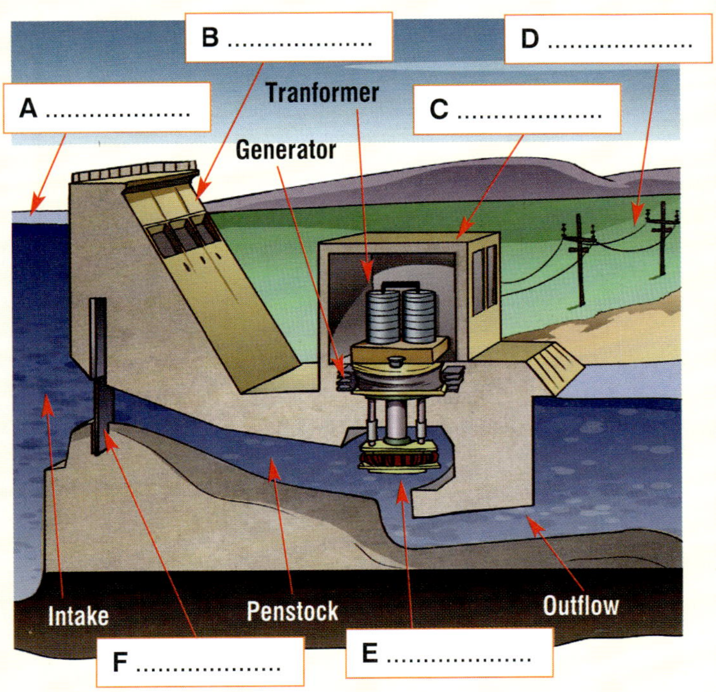

4 **Fill in:** *consumption*, *pace*, *ceremony*, *bypass*, *border*, *facility*.

1 The workers changed the course of the river by digging a .... around the construction site.

2 Work on the dam was being done at an amazingly fast ....

3 Nearly 20% of Brazil's energy .... needs is covered by the Itaipu Dam.

4 A hydroelectric power .... uses the force of water to generate electricity.

5 The Itaipu Dam lies on the .... between Brazil and Paraguay.

6 The opening .... for the dam took place on November 5, 1982.

After-Reading activities

5 **Complete the sentences using information from the text.**

The ITAIPU DAM in Numbers

1 The man-made reservoir behind Itaipu Dam spans an area of ....

2 The dam is able to produce an impressive .... of energy.

3 Each of the twenty generators in the power station has a width of ....

4 The workers had to remove .... of earth and rock from the site.

5 Every second, ... of water can flow through the turbines.

6 During the brief period the facility stopped working in 2009, ... of power was lost.

6 **Use the verbs below in the right form to write a paragraph summarizing the events that took place during the 2009 blackout.**

- restore • plunge • occur • affect
- disrupt • result in

The North Sea Protection Works

Word Bank

(pp. 26-27)

complex (adj) = complicated

series (n) = a number of things

dike (n) = a wall built to hold back water and prevent it from flooding an area

storm barrier (phr) = a barrier which protects an area from rising water levels

floodgate (n) = a structure that opens and closes and is used to control the flow of water

force (n) = power, intensity

hazard (n) = danger

major (adj) = very big

settle (v) = to go and live somewhere permanently

overcome (v) = to defeat

threatening (adj) = likely to cause damage

possess (v) = to have

defense (n) = an action taken to protect someone or something

phase (n) = a stage

vital (adj) = extremely important

literally (adv) = actually

shallow (adj) = not deep

address (v) = to deal with

draw up (phr v) = to prepare something in writing

dump (v) = to drop

mound (n) = a pile

(pp. 28-29)

mouth (n) = the part of a river where it joins the sea

delta (n) = an area of low flat land where a river spreads into many smaller ones before flowing into the sea

come up with (phr v) = to think of

safeguard (v) = to protect

make a living (phr) = to earn money by working

storm surge (phr) = a rise in the sea level caused by a storm

freshwater lake (phr) = a lake whose water is not salty

conquer (v) = to overpower

global warming (phr) = an increase in the Earth's temperature

estimate (n) = an approximate calculation

effective (adj) = successful, producing results

Pre-Reading activities

1 **a) Complete the sentences with the phrases below.**

• storm surges • freshwater lake • two phases • global warming • shallow bay

1 The North Sea Protection Works project is made up of ....

2 The Zuiderzee used to be a ....

3 Today there is a .... where the Zuiderzee once was.

4 The Maeslant barrier protects the area against the threat of ....

5 .... is making it necessary for the Works to continue improving.

b) Listen, read, and check.

While-Reading activities

2 **Replace the words/phrases in bold in the sentences below with the words in the box.**

• possess • conquer • vital • vast • safeguards • came up with • addressed • hazards

1 The North Sea Protection Works project consists of a **huge** group of different structures.

2 The problem of flooding in the Zuiderzee area was first **dealt with** in the 17th century.

3 People in the Netherlands had to find a way to protect themselves from the **dangers** associated with frequent flooding.

4 The Maeslant Barrier is a gate that **protects** the port of Rotterdam and the surrounding areas from floods.

5 The North Sea Protection Works project shows that people can **overpower** the forces of nature, to some extent.

6 The engineers working on the Delta Works **thought of** the idea of a barrier that wouldn't prevent local fishermen from going out into the open sea to do their fishing.

7 Before the 20th century, people did not **have** the technology to create major flood protection systems.

8 The constant improvement of the North Sea Protection Works is **extremely important** for the Netherlands.

3 **SUBJECT-SPECIFIC VOCABULARY: Do the crossword puzzle.**

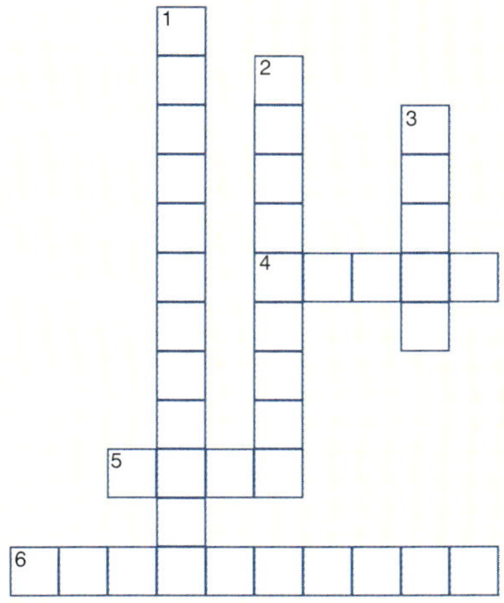

Across

4 an area of low flat land where a river spreads into many smaller ones before flowing into the sea

5 a wall built to hold back water and prevent it from flooding an area

6 a rise in the sea level caused by a storm

Down

1 a structure which protects an area from rising water levels

2 a structure that opens and closes and is used to control a flow of water

3 the part of a river where it joins the sea

4 **What can be understood about the future of the Works?**

A Environmental factors will make their continuous improvement necessary.

B They will make it more difficult for fishermen to do their work.

C They will continue to be as effective as they are today.

D It will become less costly and time-consuming to improve them.

After-Reading activities

5 **Fill in:** *major*, *dump*, *estimates*, *living*, *complex* **and** *phases* **in order to complete the summary of the chapter.**

The North Sea Protection Works is a **1)** .... system of structures protecting the Netherlands from **2)** .... flooding. It is made up of two **3)** ....: The Zuiderzee Works and the Delta Works. The Zuiderzee Works began in 1927, when ships were used to **4)** .... huge amounts of dirt, sand and other natural materials to create a dam that isolated the North Sea from the Zuiderzee. The Delta Works barrier was built in a way that it prevents flooding, but still allows the fishermen to continue making their **5)** .... by letting fishing boats pass through. Though the project is an amazing success, **6)** .... of the rise in sea levels show that it is necessary to continue developing the structures.

The Panama Canal

Word Bank

(pp.30-31)

right (n) = official permission to do or have something

landscape (n) = a particular type of land

dense (adj) = thick

rocky (adj) = having a lot of rocks

extensive (adj) = large-scale

excavation (n) = digging

rugged terrain (phr) = rough ground

take over (phr v) = to get in charge of something for which someone else was previously responsible

process (n) = a series of actions

(pp. 32-33)

invest (v) = to spend money on something in order to benefit more from it

sanitation (n) = keeping an area clean and healthy

dam (v) = to build a dam across a river or a lake

masterpiece (n) = a very skillful piece of work

valley (n) = a lower area of land between two mountains, often with a river running through it

passageway (n) = a narrow pass

rail-mounted (phr) = moving on train tracks

steam shovel (phr) = a machine used for digging the ground that runs on the hot gas produced by boiling water

carry out (phr v) = to perform a task

ahead of schedule (phr) = earlier than planned

currently (adv) = at present

transit (v) = to travel through

break out (phr v) = to begin

Pre-Reading activities

1 **a) Decide if the statements are *T* (true) or *F* (false).**

1 The French thought that building the Panama Canal would be a very expensive project. ....
2 The Americans' design of a canal was quite different to what the French proposed. ....
3 Many construction workers died because of mysterious illnesses. ....
4 The Americans used an existing valley to make part of the canal. ....
5 Eventually, the Panama Canal project was way over budget. ....
6 There are plans to make additions to the canal. ....

b) Listen, read, and check.

While-Reading activities

2 **Choose the correct option.**

1 The Panama Canal was completed in
A 1881. B 1914.

2 In order to start the construction of the canal, the US President at the time bought
A equipment from France. B materials from France.

3 The French attempts to build the canal were unsuccessful because the engineers
A found it impossible to build such a long canal.
B found the type of land in the area difficult to work on.

4 When the Americans took charge of the project, they
A suggested building a different type of canal.
B thought of a way to simplify the excavation process.

5 The Americans
A improved working conditions for the employees on the project.
B employed more people than the French.

6 The Gaillard Cut is
A a man-made passage through a mountain.
B the name of the lake created after damming the Charges River.

7 The Panamax is
A the name of the largest ship that can sail through the Panama Canal today.
B a name given to the dimensions showing the maximum size of a ship allowed to pass through the canal.

3 Choose the correct item.

1 Steam shovels were used for the **excavation/ sanitation** of the land during the making of the Panama Canal.

2 The **dense/rugged** terrain of the area made it very difficult to dig the ground.

3 Nearly a month after World War I **broke out/ carried out** in Europe, the first ship sailed through the Panama Canal.

4 An artificial **valley/landscape** was created in order to make a passageway.

5 Works on the Panama Canal finished two years ahead of **process/schedule**.

6 A great amount of money was **transited/ invested** in providing suitable working conditions for the construction crews.

4 Fill in: *rights*, *masterpiece*, *damming*, *rocky*, *currently*, *taking*, *extensive*.

1 The American engineers wanted to create a man-made lake by .... the Chagres River.

2 ...., plans are being made in order to do more work on the Panama Canal.

3 Keeping the canal at sea level meant .... digging of the hard ground.

4 The USA acquired the .... to build the Panama Canal in 1904.

5 As the proposed location for the canal was full of thick jungles and .... mountains, the engineers knew they had a difficult task ahead of them.

6 Because of the way it was created, the Gaillard Cut is thought of as an engineering ....

7 After .... over the project, the Americans spent a great deal of money on creating a healthier work environment.

After-Reading activities

5 ICT Look up more information on the Panama Canal on the Internet and complete the timeline. Use the search words: *Panama Canal timeline*.

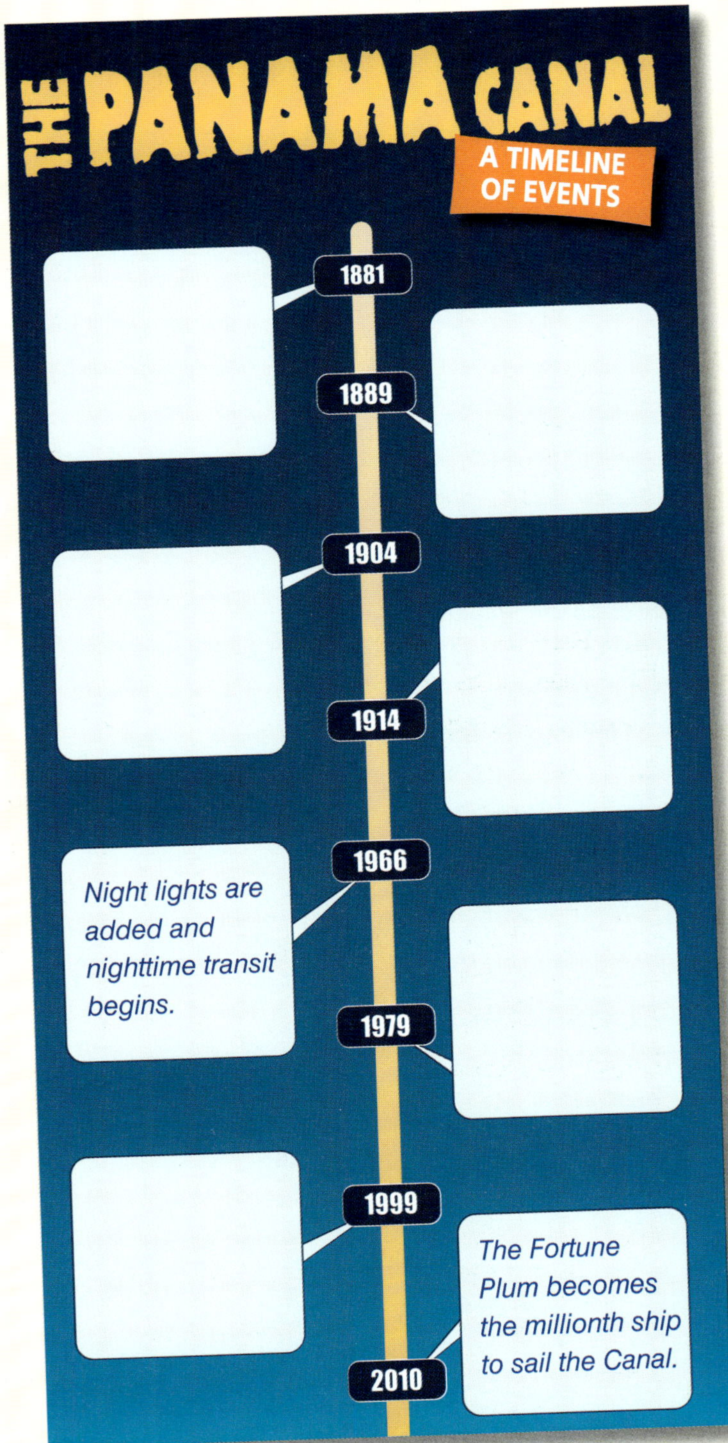

6 Use the information you collected in Ex. 5 to write a paragraph about the history of the Panama Canal.

Review

Listing Activities

1 **Listen to a dialogue about World Wonders. For questions 1-4 choose the correct answer, A, B, C or D.**

1 What are the speakers mainly discussing?

A Ancient World Wonders

B Modern World Wonders

C Engineering Wonders

D Natural Wonders

2 What did the woman think about the article she read?

A She found it confusing.

B She found it boring.

C She found it amusing.

D She found it interesting.

3 Why does the woman mention the Itaipu Dam?

A To give an example of an Engineering Wonder.

B To compare it to an Ancient World Wonder.

C To give an example of a Natural Wonder.

D To say it is the best of all Modern Wonders.

4 What does the man want to know?

A Where the woman found the article she read.

B More information on the Wonders.

C Who the American Society of Civil Engineers is.

D How The Empire State Building was built.

2 **Listen to a talk about the Itaipu Dam. For questions 1-4 choose the correct answer, A, B, C or D.**

1 What is the talk mainly about?

A The effects building the dam had on the local area.

B A comparison between the Itaipu Dam and other hydroelectric power plants.

C A description of how the dam works.

D The history of the Itaipu Dam project.

2 How did building the dam influence the people in the area?

A It gave them the opportunity to start new businesses.

B It made living in the area more difficult.

C It forced them to leave their homes.

D It created more farmland for them to work on.

3 Why does the speaker ask "But was it all bad news?"?

A To find out what the audience think on the subject.

B To introduce the next section of his talk.

C To say there is new information about the dam.

D To emphasize how bad building the dam was for the area.

4 What does the speaker say about the Brazilian and Paraguayan governments?

A Their efforts to save the local environment were not enough.

B They should have replanted more forests.

C They did more harm than good to the environment.

D They managed to rescue many species of wildlife.

Reading Activities

1 **Mark the sentences as *T* (true) or *F* (false). Correct the false statements.**

1 The CN Tower was built in order to house television channels and radio stations. ....

2 It took less than four years to complete the CN tower. ....

3 The SkyPod is the smaller of the two observation decks on the CN Tower. ....

4 Over a million people visit the CN Tower every year. ....

5 The first plans for an underwater link between England and France appeared at the beginning of the 19th century. ....

6 The Channel Tunnel was built at a much lower cost than what it was originally expected. ....

7 The construction of the Empire State Building took a little over two years. ....

8 Before the Empire State Building, there was no other building that had over 100 stories. ....

9 The Empire State Building stopped being the tallest building in the world in the early 1970s. ....

10 The Golden Gate Bridge is the world's longest suspension bridge. ....

11 Charles Ellis was the chief engineer of the Golden Gate Bridge. ....

12 The number of workers who died during the construction of the bridge was a record low at the time. ....

13 The dams that form the Itaipu complex are made from different materials. ....

14 The Itaipu Dam provides most of the electricity needed in Brazil. ....

15 During the dam's 2009 failure, Paraguay was without power for six hours. ....

16 The Dutch government could not do anything about the problem of flooding in the Netherlands before the 20th century, because it did not have enough money. ....

17 The Zuiderzee Works began in 1421. ....

18 The Maelslant Barrier is permanently closed. ....

19 The American proposal for how the Panama Canal should be constructed differed from that of the French. ....

20 The Gailard Cut is a man-made passageway cut out of a mountain. ....

2 **Write ten *T*/*F* statements based on the reader. Swap with a partner and answer them.**

Subject-Specific Vocabulary

Components of structures: counterweight, wind tunnel, pod, antenna, foundation, mast, anchor point, suspender cables, deck, support towers, main cable, transmission line, control gate, reservoir, turbine, generator, powerhouse, dam, storm barrier, floodgate, dike
Verbs: broadcast, erect, block, dig, reinforce, pump, pour, lay, maintain, leak, cave in, rivet, extend, span, suspend, generate, redirect, install, activate, estimate, transit
Nouns & phrases: engineer, civil engineering, concrete, break the record, copper wire, steel bar, wireless signals, data, pod, observation deck, elevator, staircase, observatory, rail system, diameter, ventilation shaft, sea bed, drill, boring machine, debris, over budget, frame, structural engineer, mouth, delta, power facility, storm surge, excavation, steam shovel

1 Choose the correct item.

1 **Transmission lines/Support towers** carry the energy produced in a power facility to where it is needed.
2 Both the English and the French used the **frames/debris** from the construction of the Channel Tunnel to create new areas.
3 The emergency **staircase/elevator** of the CN Tower is made up of 2,579 steps.
4 The **reservoir/powerhouse** behind the Itaipu Dam has a surface of 521 square miles and can store over a trillion cubic feet of water.
5 The **mouth/delta** of a river is the part of it where it flows out into the sea.
6 The Maeslant Barrier is a **dike/floodgate** that opens and closes to allow fishing boats access to the sea.
7 The **ventilation/excavation** of the Isthmus of Panama was difficult because of the area's rugged terrain.
8 The **copper wires/main cables** from which the Golden Gate Bridge hangs are more than 3 feet in diameter.
9 Visitors to the Empire State Building can enjoy beautiful views from the **observatories/masts** on the 86th and 102nd stories.
10 People can walk around the roof of the CN Tower's main **wind tunnel/pod** 1,168 ft above the ground.

2 Use the appropriate verbs from the Subject-Specific Vocabulary box to solve the crossword puzzle.

Across
3 to produce
4 to keep in good condition
6 to put in place
7 to make longer
8 to change the direction of something

Down
1 to raise
2 to transmit
5 to hang

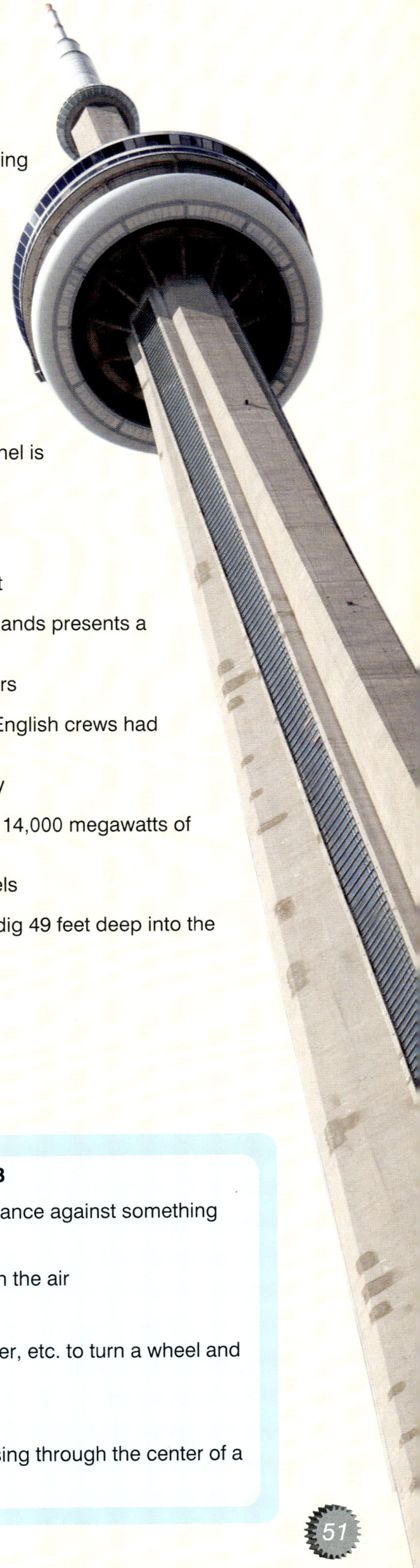

3 Choose the correct item.

1 The CN Tower .... the record as the world's tallest free-standing building in 1976.
   A obstructed   B broke
   C reinforced

2 The job of a .... engineer is to examine buildings in order to find out whether there are any problems in the way they have been constructed.
   A budget   B civil
   C structural

3 One of the eleven huge .... machines used to make the Channel Tunnel is still buried under the channel.
   A boring   B steam   C drill

4 About 13,000 ships .... the Panama Canal every year.
   A pour   B activate   C transit

5 The increase in water levels that is caused by storm .... in the Netherlands presents a serious threat of flooding for the coastal areas.
   A surges   B dams   C barriers

6 When construction of the Channel Tunnel began, the French and the English crews had planned to meet below the .... in the middle of the English Channel.
   A deck   B seabed   C facility

7 The enormous hydroelectric .... at the Itaipu Dam can produce up to 14,000 megawatts of electric power.
   A shafts   B generators   C shovels

8 In order to .... the foundations for the CN Tower, the workers had to dig 49 feet deep into the ground.
   A rivet   B pump   C lay

4 Match the words in column A to their definitions in column B.

Column A

1 turbine
2 diameter
3 antenna
4 counterweight
5 wireless signal
6 frame

Column B

A a heavy object that provides balance against something that is equally heavy
B a radio wave that is sent through the air
C an aerial
D a machine that uses steam, water, etc. to turn a wheel and produce electricity
E the basic structure of a building
F the length of a straight line passing through the center of a circular object

Speaking & Writing Activities

- **The CN Tower**

1 **Work in pairs. Imagine that you live in Toronto, and your partner is a friend from abroad visiting you. You want to take your friend on the EdgeWalk, but he/she doesn't know what it is. Explain to your partner what the EdgeWalk is and why it would be exciting to do it. Act out a dialogue.**

2 **Write a short paragraph about the history of the construction of the CN Tower. Include the words:** *foundations*, *bombsight*, *wind tunnel*, *counterweights*, *helicopter*.

- **The Channel Tunnel**

1 **Present to the class the three proposals that were not considered as suitable ways to link England and France. Choose one of these proposals that you think would have been a good idea to construct and explain the reasons for your choice.**

2 **Imagine that you were a businessperson in the early 90s and had to make frequent trips between England and France by plane or ferry. Write a letter to a friend abroad about how it felt using the Channel Tunnel to make the same trip for the first time.**

- **The Empire State Building**

1 **Work in pairs. Exchange questions with your partner to find out the information necessary to complete the fact file on the Empire State Building.**

The EMPIRE STATE BUILDING in numbers

Height:	
Number of stories:	
Number of years as tallest building in the world:	
Number of workers employed:	
Time it took complete:	
Official opening date:	
Number of visitors each year:	

2 **Write a paragraph comparing the two skyscrapers: The Empire State Building and the CN Tower. Include information about the reasons why each was constructed, differences/similarities in building techniques and other details, such as cost, time of completion, etc.**

- **The Golden Gate Bridge**

1 **Work in pairs. Prepare a *Yes/No* quiz by writing ten questions based on the chapter. Swap papers with your partner and answer each other's questions.**

2 **Answer the questions using the information from the chapter. Use your own words as much as possible.**

1 How many times has the bridge closed in all its years of operation, and why?

....

2 What made the working conditions of the construction crews difficult?

....

3 How did Joseph Strauss improve working conditions?

....

4 Why is the bridge painted in this color?

....

5 What is the weather in the bridge area often like?

....

6 Where does the money from the toll people pay to use the bridge go?

....

• The Itaipu Dam

1 **Imagine that you visited the Itaipu Dam as a tourist. Describe your experience to the class.**

2 **Complete the sentences.**

1 The four structures that make up the Itaipu Dam are: ....

2 The amount of power the dam can produce is as much as ....

3 Work on the dam began by ....

4 After the workers finished pouring the concrete needed to raise the dam, they ....

5 The 2009 blackout was probably caused by ....

• The North Sea Protection Works

1 **Explain to the class what the Maelslant Barrier is and why it was necessary to construct a structure of this type rather than a standard dam.**

2 **Match the beginnings of the sentences to their endings.**

1		Before the 20th century, there was no
2		Flooding of the Zuiderzee in 1421 resulted in
3		The Zuiderzee dam was created using
4		IJsselmeer is the lake that now exists
5		It has been recommended that the Works need
6		The Delta Works project was completed in

A dirt, sand, stones and tree branches.

B more improvements in order to remain effective.

C more than forty years.

D suitable technology to create something as major as the North Sea Protection Works.

E where the Zuiderzee bay once was.

F the loss of 10,000 lives.

• The Panama Canal

1 **Explain to the class how the Panama Canal works.**

2 ICT **Look up information on the Internet to write a short paragraph on the plans to expand the Panama Canal. Use the search phrase: *Panama Canal expansion*.**

Reading in Context

Pre-Reading activities

1 **a) Read the title of the text and look at the pictures. Why do you think these structures were given this title?**

b) Listen, read and check.

MONUMENTS OF THE MILLENNIUM

As the whole world was looking forward to the year 2000 and the beginning of the 21st century, the American Society of Civil Engineers decided to draw up a new list of engineering feats: the Monuments of the Millennium. Built in the 20th century, these structures not only show great skill and innovation in the way they were designed and built, but also had a huge positive impact on the life of the communities where they are located.

One structure on the list is Japan's Kansai International Airport in Osaka. The idea behind a new airport in Osaka appeared out of the city's need to increase the number of people and business the city received. However, building a new airport in such a heavily populated city would add to the already serious problem of high noise pollution. So, the engineers came up with the perfect solution: an offshore airport. This was the most expensive public project in modern history. An artificial island measuring 2.5 miles (4 kilometers) in length and 4,000 feet (1.2 kilometers) in width – the word's biggest man-made island at the time – was created to accommodate the world's first international airport that floated out in the middle of the sea. Kansai International Airport is 3 miles (5 kilometers) from the shore of Osaka, and is connected to the land with Sky Gate Bridge, currently the world's longest double-decker bridge.

Another impressive project that made the Monuments of the Millennium list is the Hoover Dam. Located in Black Canyon, near Las Vegas, the ambitious project was an attempt to control the wild Colorado River so as to bring water and electricity to the Southwest part of the US. The 726-ft (221-m) tall dam was initially considered impossible to construct, because of the enormous size and cost of the project. Despite early concerns, though, the Hoover Dam was completed in less than five years – two years earlier than planned – and was well under budget. When the dam opened in 1935, it boasted of being the largest of its kind at that time. Today, it no longer holds that title, but it is still the largest concrete dam in the Western Hemisphere.

The Hoover Dam

Kansai International Airport

Word Bank

skill (n) = expertise

innovation (n) = a breakthrough

impact (n) = effect

heavily populated (phr) = (of an area) having many people living there

noise pollution (phr) = harmful levels of noise in an environment

offshore (adj) = away from the coast

accommodate (v) = to provide space for sth

float (v) = to stay on the surface and not sink

double-decker (adj) = having two levels

ambitious (adj) = needing a lot of effort and skill to succeed

initially (adv) = at first

enormous (adj) = huge

concern (n) = worry

boast (v) = to speak proudly of one's achievements

While-Reading activities

2 Check the part of the sentence which is true.

1 The Monument of the Millennium is a list of structures

A ☐ that were built in the 21st century.

B ☐ that had a great influence on people's lives.

2 One of the concerns about building Kansai International Airport in Osaka was

A ☐ the fact that it would increase the levels of noise in the city.

B ☐ the fact that it would cost too much to build.

3 Kansai International Airport was built

A ☐ 2.5 miles off the coast of Osaka.

B ☐ 3 miles off the coast of Osaka.

4 The Hoover Dam cost

A ☐ rather more than what was expected.

B ☐ less than what was originally planned.

5 The Hoover Dam

A ☐ was the biggest concrete dam constructed at that time.

B ☐ took two years to complete.

3 Fill in: *initially*, *double-decker*, *boasts*, *accommodate*, *impact*, *heavily*, *ambitious*, *offshore*.

1 The city of Osaka was not suitable to .... such a large airport.

2 Given the conditions and resources of the time, building a dam that would control the Colorado River was a very .... plan.

3 Sky Gate is the name of the .... bridge that joins Kansai International Airport to the mainland.

4 People were worried about the environmental .... of building a new airport in Osaka.

5 Sky Gate Bridge .... of being the longest bridge of its kind in the world.

6 Osaka is a .... populated city.

7 Kansai International Airport was the first .... airport in the word.

8 The Hoover Dam was .... considered too expensive to build.

After-Reading activities

4 Choose the option that makes the best alternative title for the text.

A Well-structured Societies

B Innovations of the 21st Century

C Life-changing Constructions

5 ICT Find information on another Monument of the Millennium online. Write a small paragraph presenting this monument. Use the search phrase: *monuments of the millennium*.

Amazing facts

Did you know?

Until December 1970, not only vehicles but also pedestrians had to pay a 2) .... to use the Golden Gate Bridge.

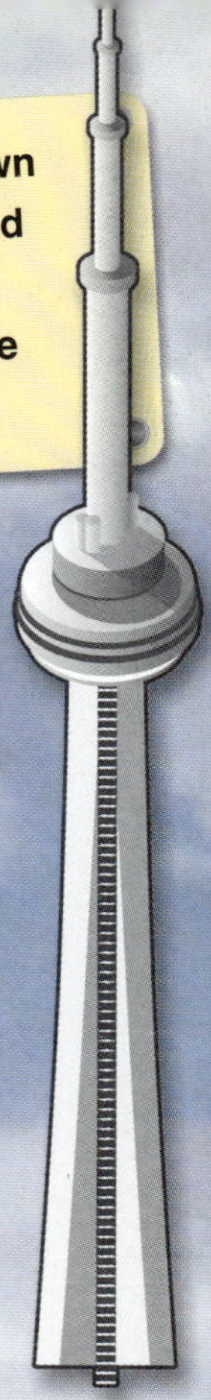

The CN Tower turns down outside lights during bird migration seasons to ensure birds have a safe 1) ....

Since 1997, more than 17 million people have visited the Itaipu Dam to take a 3) .... around one of the world's largest hydroelectric power stations.

The Zuiderzee 4) .... was formed in 1287, when the 5) .... that held back the North Sea were damaged and water flooded the farmland in the area.

The amount of material removed from the site during 6) .... works of the Panama Canal would be enough to bury the whole island of Manhattan under 12 feet of earth.

Each of the 11 7) .... that were used in the construction of the Channel Tunnel had the same length as two soccer fields.

Every year, the Empire State Building holds the Run-Up, a 8) .... in which hundreds of athletes compete to see who will be the fastest to run up the 1,576 steps to the 86th floor.

1. **Fill in:** *dikes*, *race*, *tour*, *boring machines*, *excavation*, *toll*, *flight*, *bay*.

2. **ICT Do an online search to find out one more interesting fact about each of the Seven Engineering Wonders of the Modern World. Present the facts to the class.**